NEW LOOK

Walls

Henry Pluckrose
Photography by Steve Shott

Watts Books
London • New York • Sydney

Let's begin with a thought.
Walls are everywhere.
Some walls are made
of brick or stone.

Some walls are made
of glass and steel ...

and some are made of wood.

Some walls are even growing.

Walls support the roofs of buildings.

The walls of a house protect us from bad weather ...

and give us space
to eat and sleep and play.

This wall has been built
to keep people out ...

and these walls have been built
to keep this horse in one place.

Some walls are built
for decoration ...

and some to let in
light and warmth.

Some walls have been built
to give protection –
like the walls of this castle.

Some walls are built
to contain water.

Sometimes we need to go through a wall.
We use a door to go out of a house ...

and a gate to go into a garden.

A window lets us look through a wall.
It also lets light into the building.

Walls have two sides.
Outside walls are rough and hard.

Inside walls are often decorated.

A wall has a top –
and a bottom.

What is a wall to a spider —
might not be a wall to you.

We are always building walls —

and knocking them down!

About this book

This book has been prepared for use in the home, playgroup, nursery and infant school.

The world in which young children grow and develop is a fascinating place. New experiences – things tasted, touched, heard, smelt and seen – crowd one upon another. Such experiences are the key to understanding, for their very richness and diversity fosters curiosity and encourages questioning.

We express our discoveries, our ideas and our thoughts through words. Without language, thoughts could not be shared nor ideas deepened and clarified. This marriage of words with first-hand experience is one of the keys to intellectual development.

Children view the world from a different eye level to adults yet spend their formative years in an environment specifically created for adults. This book, along with its companions in the series, is a visual exploration of everyday life from the child's viewpoint. The photographs and the text encourage talk and personal discovery – both vital elements in the learning process.

Henry Pluckrose

About the author

Henry Pluckrose is a very well known educationalist and respected author of many information books for young people. He is a former primary school headmaster who is now an educational consultant for different organisations at home and abroad.

Additional photographs:
Chris Fairclough 2
Brighton Sea World 14

© 1996 Watts Books

Watts Books
96 Leonard Street
London EC2A 4RH

Franklin Watts Australia
14 Mars Road
Lane Cove
NSW 2066

UK ISBN: 0 7496 1893 2

10 9 8 7 6 5 4 3 2 1

Editor: Annabel Martin
Design: Mike Davis

A CIP catalogue record for
this book is available from
the British Library

Dewey Decimal
Classification: 600

Printed in Malaysia